AF251861

THE NEXT CRYSTAL TEXT

▽ ∞ ✳

MELISSA MACK

▽ ∞ ☀

2017 Creative Commons BY-SA

Melissa Mack

Timeless, Infinite Light
4799 Shattuck Ave
Oakland, CA 94609

ISBN 978-1-937421-26-7

First Edition

The Next Crystal Text *was selected as the winner
of Timeless, Infinite Light's 2017 Book Contest by
Melissa Buzzeo, Mg Roberts, and Divya Victor.*

Printed by McNaughton & Gunn
Distributed by Small Press Distribution

timelessinfinitelight.com

THE NEXT CRYSTAL TEXT

FORMATION

I guess you could think of them as alive because they're forming.

Really doe, like really doe

They don't speak but have télésie body, fluoresce authentic
invisible but more energetic, metamorph
on contact. A meraviglia is born in the river of the gem-
bearing bed behind the brushwood weir.
In the 7-11 parking lot out back by the dumpster.
Practice this bearing with determination and a courageous heart.
Crystal skin is first sharp then smoothed to sugarloaf cabochon,
in the finest water with the others. In the illam.
Scooped by the barefoot kanesema with shriveled skin,
alluvial washing agent inundation.
Sieved buddled submitted sold on the street
set on the lead lap of the lapidary, held
in the drun with a pedal and a slip-roped bow.
Slotted props cradle a wooden spindle.
What were we looking *for?*
Polishing pigeon blood to prevent parting.
Working with awareness of weakness we assuage the met planes,
as in nacrine, blent in one soft blaze.
Craize late on perception of better fire from cutting.
A diamond *is* rough. It cuts to imply water.

A spark becomes a thorn becomes an ear of corn,

stone spinel, sharp crystal.

The crystal stands for something. Many

many hard days' nights.

Serried rows of myriads made

in places, directly from the matrix.

The crystal has voluptuous immobility. After the hand is taken
from the fat.

When they get up in each other's business, that's aggregate.

Physical earth reveals itself as persons.

A spark   *thorn corn spinel crystal*   becomes a fire-work.

A relation, dispersion.

We see what the crystal's electrons reject / the rejected emits.

A gleaning habit of being, to be / hold the outcast color.

It would have sounded more formal to say 'to have beheld
            the outcast'
but that makes it perfect and as Kanye says, and Nina Simone
            before him, ain't nobody perfect.

"belated and dysphoric disclosures of complicity"

A space in the atomic structure of a crystal, caused by a missing
atom, can form a color center.

                an Adam goes missing from the garden in the Eve

A crystal color center (in motherwords, a myth) is born.

          seeps into the groundwater and comes up roses

The actual work

Crystals have habits.
Subjectivity sallies from beneath their little wimpels   ~

A habit of being acicular, needle-like, slender, and tapered. A habit of being bladed.

> after the blade the blow the blood
> before the blood the flower … [*flourish*]

A habit of being coxcomb, like a bait ball of spinning fish. In the texture is the likeness. In the water is the Loch Ness.

A habit of being drusy, aggregate of minute crystals coating a surface or cavity. Lil Wayne's teeth.

A habit of being enantiomorphic, the mirror-image habit, from ancient Greek ἔναντα, facing, "in a hostile sense." *No!* Fuck longing. This is why we read the Iliad.

A habit of being filiform, hair-like or thread-like, extremely fine. Filament. Filament. Filament.

A habit of being granular, sugary aggregates of anhedral crystals in the matrix. San Francisco sidewalks.

A habit of being with hopper crystals, cubic but outer portions of cubes grow faster than inner portions creating a concavity :: A habit of being igloo-like.

A habit of being like jealousy, all features denote failure on your part.

A habit of being interlockingly kidney-shaped, collops of deli cutlets arranged on tray messily.

A habit of being lamellar, layered in thin sheets, folio-like yo.

A habit of being mammillary, breast-like, it feeds.

A habit of being nodular or tuberose, a deposit of roughly spherical form with irregular tuberose-like protuberances.

A habit of being octahedral, two pyramids base to base. How one might like to sleep sometimes, when there's another pyramid in the bed.

A habit of being prismatic, Jem & the Holograms-like elongate crystal faces parallel to well-developed c-axis.

The quizzical habit: I'm not sure where you're going with that.

A habit of being reticulated, crystals forming net-like intergrowths. Spidery elegance that's left after taxes.

A habit of being stalactitic, forming as stalactites or stalagmites, cone-shaped. Ice cream. Habit of being disrupted by sweet-themed day-dreams.

A habit of being tetrahedral, mmm, tetrahedral-shaped.

A habit of being ultra-violet when viewed through the opposing spectrum stone.

A habit of being vernacular – understood only by those with nurses who don't speak Latin.

A habit of being wheat-sheafed, aggregates resembling hand-reaped wheat sheaves.

A habit of being X-shaped, kitty-corner twinning.

A habit of being yogurt-like, indistinct.

The last and final habit, the zephyr habit. She's like the wind.

They've got all the time in the world, so they're thorough.

The actual work of mining

And yet   and yet and yet and yet and yet and yet
        with all of this *aspect* —

    the hard thing

    is the crystal

        it's hard to concentrate
                        further (unless you're opal, only, when *it*
                                loses its water it loses its fire)

Strong like a bomb, quick like a comet, can I get a word from Mr. Muhammed
As in are you there God it's me, Margaritifera margaritifera.

the mountain tries to help
     she releases her vapor
                aromatic smoke slips up through the blowhole
in the skull

and the crystal
                                                .
.

            ⚹.
           .⚹.

                   ⚹
              . . . .

                              ⚹⚹
                        . . . .

                 begin

the long time of the coming into being of the crystal
   which includes
                         awareness
accruing
   accreting
      a wearing
        a wearing

it's a cycle, but we're not at the end yet

selfish shellfish insertion

tongue, tell us
why are we so hot and wet reading

about pearl formation?

because, said the tongue,

the oyster licks her

Pilgrims would pour oil into the reliquary through the hole in the top; the oil would touch the relics, then flow out the side holes into ampullae — ritual vessels that the pilgrims would carry home, bearing tacit blessing. Oil flows, ῥέω (rhéo). Is ferried, φέρω (phéro) out to another by little vessel. Some crystals came from liquid. Have you seen an egg white dry to glossy brittle spangles? But since, they have become themselves. Don't flow. They must be ῥήγνυμι (rhégnumi), wrecked, to be moved.

"These are exactly what you think they are. Notes that don't bring happiness…"

EXTRACTION

Barbarism colors the entire picture.

Lewis Mumford

You're like, Stephanie, duh. Me too, but! The particulars!

Stephanie Young

That which is born,
the drone
   of the burthen echoes
this Dis this Dis this Dis
Waste earth burden
covers dirt will make him rich,
this deposit carried in the berth.
~~Only~~ here can we
depose it. Compose a chorus
that murder been borne
This Dis this Dis this Dis

A few facts about extraction:

A place in the ground where many gems are found is called a *deposit*.
A deposit being worked is called a *mine*.
Non-gem bearing rock in a deposit is called *deaf*.

The *spoils* of the deposit get a bitter little lexicon:

> *gangue, gob piles, culm banks, tailings, chat, slag, gyp stacks, bullion,
> slickens, slurry*

mindstuff bound to silver &

Looking at search results from search term "gemstone mining" on the *New York Times* archive, they're all about either violence in regions where the gems come from or about fashion — minus mining.

The actual work of mining, precisely because it was meant to be burdensome, was not improved during the whole of antiquity, from the earliest traces of it down to the fall of the Roman Empire.

After reaching into the basket with my eyes closed and pulling out
the leopard-spot jasper, which the woman at Angel Light said was
for intense focus on a project but staying silent about it while it's
being "stalked."

Never expose celluloid items to heat or solvents. It could be
dangerous to both you and your collectible.

It's so clear – these pretty things, they come from somewhere – but we let them be emblem.

Ear ornaments in feathers and beetle wing cases (Ecuador. Victoria and Albert Museum, London).

Through a glass darkly will never stop being a great phrase even when there's no more glass. Will that happen? We'll always have sand. But one of the articles said eventually we'll have to mine landfills for certain minerals.

Up from the grave the zombie arm came, studded with chunks of crystal. According to Atelier Swarovski, we want it raw and from the undead.

To fail to recognize the ubiquity of 'mutual indebtedness' out of some sense that it deradicalizes it is to diminish our capacity to use it as resistance against the similarly ubiquitous suppression of mutual indebtedness as a mode of social relationship.

Rocks can be thought of in terms of their influence on the life of a bit and its rate of penetration.

In Myanmar, indigenous Kachin day laborers extract jade and the cost to them is a terrible rate of heroin addiction. You don't see that in the ad.

At the Smithsonian Museum of Natural History in Washington DC, the crystal and mineral collection is enormous. Case after case in room after room. Some of the specimens look incredibly delicate, like the ones with long needle-thin crystals. I wonder how they survived their own discovery.

The valuing of minerals as pristine pieces of the earth presumes a system of global relationships in which value is extracted from all over, but only recognized – and thus realized – by those in the United States and Europe.

The Revolution and its aftermath had been traumatic years for French jewelry.

Mine: blast: dump: crush: extract: exhaust...

ESTAMOS BIEN EN EL REFUGIO. LOS 33.

really, though?

At the Dumbarton Oaks museum in DC, the lid of the reliquary.
The ampullae, ritual vessels

                              What the waste became.

Ampullae, in anatomy, are dilated portions of a canal or duct, such
as of the semicircular canals of the ear. Hear.

                        Diamond-set ring in the form of a turntable
                        record player. By Jacob Arabo – 'Jacob the Jeweler'

Resin, a viscous substance of plant origin –
copal,   *rosin*
can become gem, as in *amber.*   Remember
Resin runs down canals in the plants that have it. It can be tapped.

Crystal, though, don't flow, ῥέω (rhéo)·
it must be ῥήγνυμι (rhégnumi)   wrecked

            tapped hard with a hammer

The unbroken whole 'came *culm* (what? waste) that something new
be /come.

Make a new chain.
2 Chainz *but I got a few.*

You got it down when you look like you're in pain.

Gold body chain set with amethyst and garnets (Hoxne, Britain. c. 400 AD).

To audience, unnamed cutters, sewers, embroiderers, beaders, I attribute this beauty, when meaning, i.e. style, is given a sympathetic presence.

Mystification of Columbian emeralds thus had to go an extra
step — towards fraud. Otherwise, one would have to accept that the
glorious emeralds of the shahs originated in the unjustly conquered
American colonies of Catholic Spain, were mined by forced Native
American serfs and African slaves, were carried to Asia by mostly
Jewish merchants hounded and tortured by the Inquisition, only
to be consumed by the world's most powerful and, frankly, often
despotic Muslim rulers.

Introducing the New Crystal: Where All Inclusive Is All Exclusive

Prada hair ornaments and brooches; other dress embellishments

Gucci rings; single strand of below-shoulder earrings

Chanel beetle brooch; another brooch peeking out from under the dress collar

Dolce & Gabbana shoes head phones purses phone case bracelet head band necklace barrette skirt buttons earrings necklace ring and one navette rhinestone hanging from a baby bracelet

Miu Miu parure

Sam Edelman drusied lapis-like crystal crosswise on a ring

Simone Rocha pearls surrounded by rhinestones as skirt clips and a double choker

Dior rhinestones lining the 'floor' of clear square three-inch heel on a pair of boots

Jimmy Choo drusy along the edges of sunglasses

Oscar de la Renta chandelier earrings; dress embellishment; pearl ring with jewels

Givenchy face jewels – pearls under the models' eyes and on nose lips cheeks

Brahmin pearl studs

Vince Camuto big square-cut carnelian ring

Amazon Fashion black pearl on a ring in a Trina Turk outfit

Pandora Jewelry pavé rings and earrings

Moschino pearls on a gold chain belt

Tod's square flat slab of marble or agate on a ring

Kate Spade Anh Duong sitting at a bar holding a fox wearing loafers set with big rhinestone flowers

Afghanistan lapis lazuli emerald ruby sapphire tourmaline aquamarine kunzite topaz garnet *Britain Russia U.S. Rahimullah*

Angola diamond *Portugal Pereira Tito*

Argentina rhodochrosite jade amethyst tourmaline *Spain*

Armenia amethyst carnelian garnet beryl turquoise aquamarine lapis lazuli diamond *Persian Ottoman Russian*

Australia diamond opal sapphire emerald peridot *British Dutch Dawn Peter Ivan Lucky Mick Len*

Brazil diamond emerald aquamarine topaz tourmaline amethyst chrysoberyl alexandrite *Portugal*

Chile lapis lazuli *Spain Mario Jose Victor Claudio Carolos*

Columbia emerald *Spain*

Democratic Republic of Congo diamond formerly *Belgian Congo Belgium*

Egypt emerald turquoise *Britain Thomas Mohammad Ali Aderup Naim*

Guyana diamond formerly *French Guyana France*

Madagascar emerald aquamarine tourmaline amethyst moonstone
morganite tsavorite garnet sapphire chrysoberyl *France*

Myanmar ruby spinel peridot moonstone jade sapphire *Imperial
Burma British Burma Independence Military Rule Tan Tomphei*

South Africa diamond *Britain Thobile Thabiso Anele Makhosandile
Julius Janeveke Mafolisi*

Sri Lanka ruby sapphire aquamarine tourmaline amethyst
moonstone formerly *British Ceylon Britain Sunil Watadeniya Damit Galla
Dinapaula Piasena*

Zimbabwe diamond emerald aquamarine chrysoberyl tourmaline
Company rule in *Rhodesia — British South Africa Company* (mining rights)

My closest experience, I imagine, to that of laborers working
gem-bearing river gravel in, say, Ratnapura or Balangoda in Sri
Lanka, where the rough stones cut the feet and long hours in the
river shrivels the skin, was, once, having taken a long walk around
a lake in Washington State, I wandered off the path and arrived at
the muddy edge of the shoreline. I could see the beginning of the
trail from where I stood, but the woods along the shore were too
dense for me to push through and I didn't want to go back the way
I came, being so close to where I had started. So I took off my
shoes to walk through the slag, which turned out to be a bed of
some sharp-shelled bivalve and cut my feet all up by the time I got
across. I did not really close the circle. A better example is when I
had a youth program summer job at the post office on the military
base unloading bags of mail from the trucks. Because it was
physical labor and I got strong. God, this is embarrassing. Or, no,
when I was a kid in southeastern Connecticut, playing the game
we called Fire Fire Ice Ice, part of which involved lying face-down
next to the curb on the road in the cold stream of water from the
garden hose after having lain on the hot asphalt for as long as you
could stand it. By virtue of the fact that I studied the street gravel
up close and picked out pebbles I thought were pretty.

Futility says, This is masturbatory. I reply, I masturbate! It is
important! The body as a passage-way — it lets something through.
As, lying belly down on a hot rock, what comes into you. What
goes between. I feel the rock receive me. I love it. But also I am
having trouble with my asshole and I don't want to talk about it. *an
aesthetics born of meningitis, addiction, rectal cancer.*

If I feel / I have to make an offering

Gold Minoan pendant in the form of a bee.

Bee brooch in enameled gold with plique-à-jour enamel wings and petals.

Brooch set with a carved agate cameo of Eros imprisoned, surrounded by diamonds.

ore & gold oh oh

Police shot dead 34 striking workers at the Marikana platinum
mine in South Africa. The victims were killed a week after walking
off the job in a call for higher pay.

glass or enamel coated with *essence d'orient* produced from the scales of certain fish, fish-scale pearl; part of a sea-snail shell, antilles pearl; part of a mussel shell, takara pearl; teeth of the sea cow, dugong pearl; snail slime and egg white; mother-of-pearl with gum arabic and dew; plastic

At the Hillwood Estate musuem in DC, Marjorie Merriwether Post's — of the Post/General Foods fortune — collection of Cartier jewelry was on display. I read that her response to the Great Depression was to un-insure her jewelry and open a soup kitchen. Cartier's was to start working in semi-precious stones.

Oh lord. (the way Drake says it)

Feeling absurd and out of place. Who am I to use the lingua franca of hip hop, freely appropriating from othered-into-safer-celebrity young black men. And if you don't know, this is how we errbody lifestyle antidote.

I go to Local 123, a hip café not a union hall, to work. Insert emoji of Charlie Brown: the one where his mouth is a wavy line and he gets parentheses on either side of his pencil-scrawl dot-eyes, and sometimes, in especially humiliating circumstances, an extra sort of elongated apostrophe just outside of the lower half of the parentheses. Humiliation, despair, *bearing*.

I'm lonely as fuck but I'm staying with it. Went to the de Young Museum and looked at the Mesoamerican art and Navajo blankets. A sculpture in soapstone by an Inuit artist, Abraham Anghik Ruben, of a spirit boat bearing souls to ... the next place. That it was bearing them was what held me. Later I realized that the spirit bearing them in the boat that was herself was Sedna, the sea goddess I drew from the Goddess deck with Sara and Mali.

That all of these jewelries – pins, clips, necklaces, earrings – attach to the wearer suggests the possibility of social bonding and violence at the same time.

The plane tree in the median is umber colored but the color is obscured by the white sky behind. A branch hangs two loose hooks of leaves over the street. Two hooks of leaves loose over the street. Through the glass the median trees hang their leaves over the street shaggily. Is it generosity if you don't have a choice? A baby's arms and legs – visible in my periphery – wave rhythmlessly like anemone limbs in a light undersea breeze. Current. Yes, yes it is. This is critical, because the stakes – can we have agency when trapped inside a rapacious system? – are so high. Duncan says, assuaging H.D.'s concern over her reluctance to participate in some Rosicrucian ritual with Yeats and his wife Georgie, that it was the disinterest of a growing thing for possibilities outside its law, its real. So, the other side of that 'coin' is the interest of a growing thing for possibilities inside its law. I want to believe that the trees offer themselves to the street. I do.

Broad collar composed of glazed 'faience' beads and pendants (Egypt, c. 2020 BC).

Skin heals from the inside out, Caro said –
Known in all the moments of tearing and repair –
Out of hallowed bodies bred
So, to have alone broken –
To be lifted, literally –
Took bread, ate and pray –
Friends say what life is to them - dream spray, mermaids, work –
Rhiannon, Maeve, Sedna bless the space –
While refugees. While police.
While system spins its nasty logic, its anti-magic.
But be *thou* my vision, women –

I start to cry like five times a day. "Honey," Joshua says, "tell me about it." Not as in tell me about it. As in don't we.

In the Finnish epic poem *Kalevala*, Ilmatar, goddess of ether, grows depressed and lonely in her empty airy region and so tries the sea for a change of scene. As she descends a storm rushes up. *The wind her womb awakened,* the waves surged about her and their foam made her pregnant. Or, as the 19th Century English translation chastely states, *thus she swam as water-mother.* This is only the beginning of the story. Heavy with child, she is trapped beneath the sea, which she swims for 700 years. At last she grows desperate, cries out to the god Ukko to help her. A beautiful duck appears, searching for a place to build its nest but finding none across the watery waste. Ilmatar lifts her head and shoulders and her knee out of the water. The duck builds a nest on her knee and lays seven eggs. Over the next few days, Ilmatar's knee grows warm and then burning hot with the heat of the duck's brooding. Unable to take it any longer, she thrashes her limbs and the eggs tumble into the water and crack apart. At the bottom of the sea they reassemble into the World Egg, and the lower part of the egg forms the earth and the upper the heavens, and the yolk the sun and the white the moon. She is still pregnant, by the way. *There are other words of magic, / Incantations I have learned…* The Greek word γόνυ (gonu), knee, is cognate with the words γίγνομαι (gignomai), to come into being, γένεσις (genesis!), origin, and a handful of others all related to generation. The generative joint. Filled with the fluid of life. In Ancient Chinese, rock crystal was known as water-germ (or water-sperm). The crystal the seed, the knee the nest. From storm-spiral to sweet harmony. Harmony comes from Greek ἁρμός (harmos), joint. "An articulation of the body." From Indo-European root ar- 'to fit together'. My joints do not generate harmony. They become hot and say pain. But now my knee joint is replaced with water-germ and I am not to become the mother of a human child born of my belly, having tried and tried, fancifully like Ilmatar with her swimming and with studied intent like the beautiful duck. My eggs are almost bled out, but I do bear.

Another word from the ar- root, possibly, is *order*, from Latin
ordo, originally of threads in a loom and ordiri, to begin to weave.
Hector telling Andromache to go on back to her distaff and loom,
he and the other men would worry about war. Well, OK, *I'd* rather
be weaving. I mean, not literally — the only thing I know about
weaving is the word loom. I had to look up distaff. But/and I do
know the pull to flee the scene of the battle. During the marches at
UC Davis and UC Berkeley in 2009 to protest the privatization of
a public school system, during 2010 and 2011 during the Occupy
movement, during the marches after the non-indictments of black
men's murderers in 2014 and 2017, after black men's murders in
2015 and 2016, I often rode home before the skirmishing started
with police. For one thing I am scared of cops. Duh. Also C. said
something once about Adrienne Rich, criticized for not being
politically active enough, that someone had to write the poems of
the movement, which is hard to do on the actual march. I embrace
and repudiate that over and over. See also Levertov/Duncan, his
'cosmologizing impulse', where she believed more in the physical
street. When I played softball, briefly, in junior high, in fact and in
truth I was out in left field (that meadow*), gaze on the tree line
or studying the grass intently, from dreamy belief that important
action was happening there and nervousness at being too close to
this other action, the game. Pride & shame.

*But Why do they need to preserve the privileged permission
White Supremacy gives them to return to a 'meadow'? Why are we
so happy about the Meadow?

After breakfast we took a walk up the Mandela Parkway median and
saw this bush we didn't recognize. A few fuschia blossoms, papery
like bougainvillea leaves, then big hard russet and green-gage colored
hips, then these lumpy lemon yellow fruits, and one withered on
the vine, black, like petrified ash. All on the one bush. In his reply
to the Sadducees asking Jesus this horrible hypothetical question
about a woman who had been married successively to seven brothers,
who would she be married to at the resurrection, Jesus refers to
the account of the burning bush. He doesn't mention that it was
burning. Everyone knows what bush. Our bush also had thorns.
Long needle-like ones. In the original account of the burning bush,
in Exodus, Moses first does a double-take: "here, the bush is burning
with fire, and the bush is not consumed!" Then "Moses said: Now
let me turn aside that I may see this great sight — why the bush does
not burn up!" It's only at that point — "When YHWH saw that
he had turned aside to see, YHWH called to him out of the midst
of the bush." Only when he leaves the path to really look, then G-d
spoke. G-d or the messenger of G-d. There were grass clippings
scattered around the base of our bush, like mulch or marking. After
he has turned aside to attend, Moses is warned. "Do not come near
here. Put off your sandal from your foot for the place on which you
stand is holy ground!" Does it come through, how angry I am?

The forged thing has life. Its aura is green.

Did it have life before the fire?

Yes, but

it was inert. The first fire, breath of life (more a roar),

receded. The un-forged thing waited,

practiced self-soothing breathing and yoga nidra,

lucid sleep.

Time out of mind forward came the long-legged page, the forge

attendant – the blacksmith. So light, even with its leather apron.

Its mask had glass (or plastic)

so the worker could see its trapped matter.

Easy there, it crooned, come on,

it stroked as it stoked the fire,

let us see your nature.

To identify as radical thus requires participation in communities that are dedicated to exploding the system. What's hard is saying no all the time. You have to. There's so much to say no to. But then sometimes I can't find where life is. How to say yes to love and beauty and friendship, to other forms of life?

Although you wish the answer would be yes, it isn't. The answer isn't yes.

I don't want to be in love with failure. But I don't want to "fail better" either. Fuck that Silicon Valley bullshit. I don't care if Samuel Beckett said it and Pema Chödron wrote a book about it. It's too late for me. I'd rather just fail and bear it.

You just do I don't know. You have potlucks and reading groups and prayer circles and go to commie camp and do rituals with your friends and shut down the freeway when everyone gets angry enough that another black person has been murdered by a cop and counter-intuitively it's a joy to gather and walk and listen and chant and hang out on the highway while it gets dark and the horizon glows for ages.

At the Bulgari Exhibition at the de Young Museum in San
Francisco, everything is shown about the process of making jewels
except the laborers who bring the metals and stones out of the
ground. Instead, we are immersed in a sensory fantasy. Ambient
glittery sounds fade in and out as you walk through the show.
Sparkly material lines the display cases and holographic projections
play and replay in each case. In one, a house of playing cards
collapses, in another coins fall from the 'sky' of the case, in another
a swan blows away feather by feather. After each projection finishes,
the case appears empty for a moment until side lights illuminate
one piece – a heart/spade/club/diamond brooch, a coin pendant,
swan pin. There's this moment before the side lights come on when
the viewer thinks the case is empty. Pleasant frisson of shock. Also,
haha, the trace of the dialectical image (= commodity) in the
velvet lining of their casings. In real life! On the walls surrounding
the display cases, slowly morphing virtual wallpaper, images from
the Bulgari collection and drawings of new jewelry pieces being
imagined. Images of celebrities wearing Bulgari jewels fade in
and out – the jewels showing before the celebrity body fades in
with the necklace or bracelet or watch or brooch glowing on what
reveals itself to be a famous neck or arm or waist. The last section
of the exhibit shows how loose gemstones became one particular
Bulgari jewel. The signage boasts that the viewer is being let in on
the *whole process.*

Not true!

I should really start using shampoo again.

At Jami's, I use hers and then this leave-in conditioner.

My hair feels so soft and clean and pretty.

After reading Claudia Rankine's *Citizen* again

I set the book down and put my face in my hands.

I cry my white women's tears and feel

grateful to be alone because the world

doesn't need my white women's tears.

It needs other things from me.

My face feels soft too. I had used the Pink Light

herbal face grains or whatever. They worked beautifully.

So now my hair is soft and my face clean and tear-streaked.

I have half the week off (the morning half)

and am house-sitting in this spacious quiet house

with animal companions.

There's a chord

made by my shame and culpability in this made place,

the grace and call rendered to me as evidenced by my being alive,

and the singularity of this instant.

I tune to it. It makes my skin prick.

Just like the safety-pin dress must have done to Elizabeth Hurley
when she was being pinned into it and pierced with Bulgari and
set on Hugh Grant's arm. I made myself put Hugh Grant in this
book. Banality of celebrity jewelry.

the day deepens into day

smudged putty stretched thin, shell above stone below

a day wherein the light is diffuse, the air's atoms almost visible,

enriches the heart – a dialed down diffusion, not like the Ascension

look through the yellow obsidian

first a screen then a door

                              And A Way Opened...

inner oyster shell shine

plane shone as it caught the light

it is a craft

that we should call upon ourselves to play new roles when

the time is right

At the Burke Museum of Natural History in Seattle, on the Maōri
pataka, storehouses, human figures are shown with spirals at their
hip joints and knee joints. In the kids' rocks & minerals book, it
says crystal faces are rarely planes, rather the atoms spiral. Like
Dante's cosmos, and the way he goes through it, around and down
and down and down, up and around and up and up, and up up up,
finally arriving at the center of the celestial rose, whose petals are
the souls of the blessed, *which expands and rises in ranks and exhales odors
of praise to the Sun that makes perpetual spring,* and the angels descending
and ascending into the center of the flower and up to the pure
light of God, like BEES RUSHING BETWEEN FLOWER
AND HIVE, *where their toil is turned to sweetness.* !!!!!!!!!!

The jewel the jewel
The hungry swan

Jet, the "gemstone," comes from waterlogged wood trapped under layers of mud – carbon compressed over time. Was worn for mourning.

Dangle these darlings at your throat, and you will go gleaming and glowing, lighting up the night.

Small diamond stones are called *melée*.

Breaking the fashion dictum of 1920, "No jewelry in the street!"

We,

     we come into our new being under great pressure.

charm

In my last two weeks of being 39 I did an I Ching reading
asking, "what is the crystal project really about?" My coin throw
yielded Hexagram #13, Fellowship with Men [sic], changing to
Hexagram #9, The Taming Power of the Small. Of Hex 13, the
commentaries say, crossing the great water is to cross from the
human realm to the divine realm while on earth. At which point
unheard of things become possible. Of Hex 9, that it is a time
of becoming. Becoming is not simple. The new always passes
through blood and fear. But that renunciation of existing forms
occurs by means of the utmost sincerity which causes blood and
fear to vanish. Which I doubt, but I did dream of three whales
suspended mid-leap and open-mouthed above the sea, blooming
like watermelon-flesh flowers.

This, my humiliating and ever-complicit sincerity, is my crossing.

It is necessary to notify one's own city.

[Aguilarite] became valuable by virtue of its distinction from
other silver minerals present in the Guanajuato district and, more
broadly, from all other minerals already discovered, described, and
named.… Once this happened, aguilarite became an actor in its
own right, in the sense that it could now do things.

Diadem of enameled gold set with cornelian intaglios, c. 1808, Paris

It looks light, the diadem.
It's hammered gold fashioned like a ribbon
caught in a curl, a wave formation
that ripples around, nearly full circle.
Set into the ribbon are amber cameos —
men or gods framed in blue
enamel ovals. The seals of history
anointing their chosen.
Along the edges of the golden ribbon-circlet
tiny wave forms cascade,
marked, each one
with an enamel dot at the joint — the place
where each crest begins or ends at the ribbon edge.
The ribbon crown is carved
with gestural leaf patterns and stamped
with others at the upper and lower limits —
the apex and nadir of each wave. It's ornate.
Along the center — cutting across the ribbon
waves, a horizon line
of small interlocking gold discs, each with
that dab or boss of blue enamel at its center.
A series of pinky-finger-sized shields,
well-balanced on every side.

All the accoutrements of state cooperate
in inscribing the permanence of power.
The sanction and protection. But
there is an opening.

Crossing the great water is indicated by the inner trigram Sun, which means wood and gives rise to the idea of a ship.

Pendant in the form of a ship in gold, silver, opal, tourmaline, small diamonds, and enamel.

On the ferry deck, I walk around and around, counterclockwise. In this direction it feels more like a spiral.

SETTING

The ornament is exalted.

and so prove, / As ornaments oft do, too dangerous

Scarab necklace, the oval heart scarab in glazed steatite surrounded by a diamond and onyx lotus, suspended from a pearl ribbon band.

Scarab brooch, the winged heart scarab in engraved smoky quartz with cabochon emerald eyes, the outstretched wings in antique blue faience with cabochon emeralds and striated with diamonds.

The Valentino ad with Jolly Ranchers'-colored plastic bangles and a clutch. A chevron in the resin.

Ring with a hyper-glossy lucite ice cube for a stone — so slick like liquid, your own juices generate just looking.

Diamond
Emerald
Amethyst
Ruby,

Ruby
Emerald
Garnet
Amethyst
Ruby
Diamond

Terrible
Human
Exploitation

Capital
Overburden
Slickens
Travesty   (what the waste became)

When I look at it, the deep Asscher cuts – which are so complete and so ravishing – are like steps that lead into eternity and beyond. My ring gives me the strangest feeling for beauty. With its sparks of red and white and blue and purple and on and on, really, it sort of hums with its own beatific life. To me, the Krupp says, "I want to share my chemistry – my magic – with you."

Elizabeth Taylor talking about the Krupp diamond, a 33-carat square-cut (that's the Asscher) diamond so named because it was owned by Vera Krupp, of the munitions family that helped "knock off" millions of Jews. Elizabeth Taylor said she thought, "how perfect it would be if a nice Jewish girl like me were to own it."

Make me feel some type of way.

Enter the gentyl joueler.

Come forth! Look into the loupe.

In the loupe, the inclusions. Material

there when the crystal was forming and the crystal just flowed
around it with its

voluptuous immobility, catching it up and calling it history.

Rutile, silk, gasses, fans, liquids, other crystals.

To industry, inclusion is flaw. Cuts clarity.

Grounds for exclusion. No

demand if everything is included

everyone has.

(On the other hand, some gems are "too rare to be marketable.")

But what proliferation! A limitless universe of forms.

Fabulous scapes of volcanoes, forests, cosmoses, ghosts.

Ancient beads of carnelian, chalcedony, lapis, faience, glass, and
amethyst.

twinkle sparkle
bitter figure
stones are sold
in little packets
in the market
in a jacket
all the rest
are still at rest
until the day
they are extracted
red and blue and green
and yellow
whisper to the earth
to tell you
where is the kimberlite
pipe to break open
it's raining men
it's raining diamonds
it's raining from the
ground up
you don't get a rainbow

Collets collar. Heals the neck.

A gem setting. A collection of gem settings and their inorganic flora.

A collection or collect*ing* is a good model for identity formation
because it is acquisitive, growing the being, but selective,
winnowing towards differentiation from other beings.

An assembly pared, the parure matches.

But you can break it up, wear the brooch in your hair,

give the other half to your BFF.

– for strength, for guiding, for attachment to another. The *other body!*

Strong structure has this earth
fiery mantle that haunts
It can collapse and the end
is foretold in many books
and visions that prompted their record
Is it like spider architecture?
Made and destroyed and made again
Transient tensile tinsel its material
Track a pattern and prophecy
The web will be again
The world we don't know

My tears have been my meat day and night.

My tears have been my mate night and day.

My pendaloque-cut emeralds have become emblem of the world-
        end.

RELATION

Press the surface and the skin transmits
          come up behind me
          your hammer gets fat i fracture
                              break / out / in   thin discs of

          quartz crystal

Baby, when we're grindin' I get so excited.

To celebrate is to frequent. Frequented is crowded.
Numerous is famous, more faces seen frequently.

After watching the Steven Soderberg two-part movie about Che
Guevara, *Che* – Che is played by Benicio del Toro, who's Puerto
Rican but was raised in Pennsylvania, "not much in the back pocket"
– I wonder, should I be participating in armed struggle against white
supremacist imperialist capitalist patriarchy? *(Not a joke.)*

Benicio del Toro is beautiful. I meant to say famous. Frequented.
Seen. Seen in, for. Seen as. *Of being numerous.*

If I touch it anyhow it will take in my skin / to the blaze of its own imperfections.

if the skin is lapped leaves sticky little tabs as its apparatus
til it like to burst hackle or make   the spark jump

                                        I say people (What?)

what you gonna do?

the membrane is full, then, the membrane is thin.   a when is made
– there's a condition

Through the glass from incident light

                                            sap fire could catch

as stick to other stick, wet lap electric   crystal

        it's only temporary

                                    in clusions of unusual necessity
        there's a time for twinning
a time for coloring   when the trace and then the seeing

        a time for co-embodiment, power in the house

i'm not saying i don't miss meetings

it's easier when there's space. open system pretty cavity drusied with glittery crystal. sometimes. sometimes there's too many too much and it just sucks ass and not in the way you want.

If distribution and circulation are the aspects of production that
are "properly historical," (production & consumption being *given*
by/according to need — already problematic because it's too late
to consider production & consumption givens driven by need, the
species — being in its historical moment experiencing *need* in a way
so far removed from 'that required to survive' — which we could talk
about that but for short say food, shelter, and relationship — it's not
recognizable any longer, but OK, I'll go with it for now it's not the
main point of this digression), the circulation model of the moment
we might seize is, as Lisa Robertson points out in her Untitled Essay
in *Nilling*, ecology. And we'd better care to seize it for real else the
bright light of shipwreck gonna be collective and similarly moving
as its metaphor. Moving as decomposing. Which, yeah, in a really
big picture way is how it goes and I have many days where to live is
Christ, to die is gain — *And it was morning, and it was evening, the 365 x
39 + 180-oddth day, the 365 x 41 + 300-oddth day.*   But to my point,
or, to Lisa's point that I am attaching to like a microchip of granite
aggregate, ecology as a "circulatory model of a mutually embodied
power-in-relationship, as long as one considers ecology in terms
of complex processes of disequilibrium and emergence instead
of a harmonized closure." Ugh. This is a terrible, disequilibrious
interruption and I feel miserable about it. Something I've learned
to recognize as useful and a necessary part of art. That rusty squat
equant on Georgia O'Keefe's *Jack in the Pulpit 2* from 1930 seriously
irritates me and I know that's good.

#mood

Moonstone cameo
camo for clothing my feelings
for to walk in spring to the faerie ring
for scrying school
there are benches for the humans
just like the ones the soldiers made
in the Cuban Revolution
because learning is part of the movement
there's a kitchen to make food and herbal medicine,
an open hearth
there I can heat-treat my moonstone
so it glows and the portal opens
and I can visit my grandparents
the corn and soybean farmers, the diesel mechanic, the army cook,
Give me some sugar!
and learn the summer lesson
from the snake who stays cool
in the medicine herbs and hidden
under the dandelions' straw hats
until
the time of the cycle when
festive dress become seed spears
and the moonstone camo
is for protection while fighting.

The *Gita* says, "No one should relinquish his [*sic*] duty, even though it is flawed; all actions are enveloped by flaws as fire is enveloped by smoke."

Figuring out what one's duty is is the trick.
Would you have done what Arjuna did?

it's so hard
    not to be able to say
        the sacred thing in the center
            whole hollow protected from prying eyes
            that pollen is locked up tight
                one bee can't free it
                    each bee got to hang out by the ( )
                    un-til
                    the advent is over
                what's left is the κοῖλος, the coil
            the hollow is held by the humming
        it makes a harmonic
      OM
    & then a pollen explosion and everyone has an orgasm
the secret came from its hiding place

washing agent, inundation

THE LATTICE

terror ever present / a shitty lattice
                    Ted Rees

rocked only by love, hazard, fate, sleeping —
                    Lisa Robertson

There's an angel there
Your counterpart in heaven
A counterpane that covers you
Hovers above you

~~~~~~~~~~~

The way to the angel can be seen in each tree
Its direction, motion, texture, pressure
Thicken yourself like a cat with its hair out
Rustle, shiver, glitter
Play wood duck diving from its nest
Pour toward incorporeal arms
~~~~~~~~~~~

Here's something that's already been said:
I saw a hundred little spheres which beautified each other with their mutual
                              beams.
That's the lattice.
The High Priestess walks through the underworld
From Point A to Point B. That's an imaginary
Axis. The river is another.
In this center, and many others besides, resides the sun.
And eke a hundred sonnes. . .
Who grows there through the structure with their light footfalls —
The holy androgyne,
Brilliant at each fresh cleavage.

Some of us and our invisible angels waited for the bus.

We were seeking the secret.

Like bacteria, we knew it was there

But the medium concealed it.

Black light was our second site —

We were busy beaming.

On the bus the seats were gross.

Public transit and fabric, a bad trip.

Around the corner the accordion expanded and

There, in the fold, an iridescence glowed.

Then what did the secret do? It grew.

We listen for a time, we hear silence
There is a silence of the moon and a silence of the sun
The silence of the sun is hot
Notchings and squeakings
As growing things push through this or
That joint or corpulent mandorla
The silence of the moon is wan
It recedes, and here along the littoral
See the seeds encased in juice
That cannot be released
Until the Priestess sings

Our chariot-boat knows no six-sided agony.

Through the starry sea it flees —

Feels fleet, releasing its radiance of abundance.

It has nowhere to go —

Only away, toward the end of the center.

Heeds not the hearth beneath.

It is a crosser of surfaces and wastes —

Sudden butterfly in the night sky.

Discord is its power source.

A wake behind,

It desiccates and iridesces.

The crystal is hidden in the form —
The fountain —
Not mined or mine —
Radiant —
Liquid cupola filling —
Lipped cups flowing ~~~~~
From the hood —
The hiding place —
The ornament flies —
Or stays —
According as time —

The lattice is a chalice, an ace.
Of course it is, it's LOVE.

The plant is the matter: suffer and death.
Meanwhile systems swirl and stuff awaits rebirth.

The moon is the measure.
We say it when we mean blood.

The angel tends toward us as we tend
Toward others. The angel longs
For us as light grows long.

The gong is the ring, a clang.
It conducts us, cygnets in our nest on the precipice.

The love of lovers for each other made you, stone.

Force removed you from your matrix.

It was explosive or it was by means

Of insistent hands with simple tools.

You will live for a season in this underworld

As jeweled as a pomegranate torn open.

You will be worn. You will become worn.

Wear, the oil of mourning and morning,

Grows your glory, your luster —

A still sea glowing with subtle color.

Prismatic ripples whereupon others are born or borne.

A message with weight can carry one a long way.

Let's say we're not in hell, not that we know

Of. Wherever we are, here is where the announcement is

Made and — a sequence if not a consequence — stilled.

Goodbye, Hearken. Hello, Passion.

The character to whom this happens

Is clad, her clothes cling to her for destiny.

A crab companion accompanies her.

Not for protection or to attack her, but as a token, like a brooch —

Of a plan yet to click jeweled claws —

A transmigration in wait —

We looked for a way in — it was a hidden button.
We touched it and boarded this lift.
You kissed me on the mouth and a liquid flowed in.
You were as surprised as I among the junk.
It tasted like an extension of the kiss — the kiss' natal space
Come forth with it unto me.
I don't know if the lift moved —
Sometimes you might drift before the airplane takes
Off, and wake, and not feel the being air —
Borne until you turn and find the ground is gone and
Clouds are the new signs — while we did this.

This concerns a journey.
The journey is certain. It occurs. Plural.
The pearl performs, the wanderer, ibid.
Filaments are always calling, and they catch,
But special sense lets you see them atimes.
Once (last night) I kept walking into spider silk.
In an attempt to grasp it, you say everything you can think of.
Maybe I broke through into the imaginal when
The first beaded strand met my face at a slant
And I was in it for 20 paces or years
Then broke back in or out — each time touched.

GLOSSARY

alluvial: of or relating to deposits of clay, silt, sand, and gravel left by flowing streams in a river valley or delta, typically producing fertile soil

buddle: a shallow inclined container in which ore is washed

cabochon: a gem polished but not faceted

craze: produce a network of fine cracks on (a surface)

dop: a tool for holding gemstones for cutting or polishing

illam: gem-bearing river gravel

kanesema: Burmese, female laborer who sifts river gravel for gemstones

matrix: the fine-grained portion of a rock in which coarser crystals or rock fragments are embedded

meraviglia: Italian, marvel

nacrine: of or relating to mother-of-pearl, a smooth shining iridescent substance forming the inner layer of the shell of some mollusks, especially oysters and abalones, used in ornamentation

pigeon blood: describes a vibrant and highly-valued shade of red found in rubies

spinel: a hard glassy mineral occurring as octahedral crystals of variable color and consisting chiefly of magnesium and aluminum oxides

télésie: varieties of corundum: ruby, sapphire, and yellow topaz, from the greek τέλεσις, meaning 'perfection'

weir: a low dam built across a river to raise the level of water upstream or regulate its flow

NOTES

FORMATION

"I guess you could think of them as alive because they're forming"
overheard, mother to son, Smithsonian Museum of Natural History,
Washington DC, 18 April 2014.

Really doe like really doe. Danny Brown ft. Kendrick Lamar, Ab-Soul, Earl
Sweatshirt, "Really Doe," *Atrocity Exhibition,* Warp, 2016.

as in nacrine, blent. . . Philip J. Bailey: *The Angel World and Other Poems* (Boston:
Ticknor, Reed, and Fields, 1950): 34.

Physical earth reveals itself as persons. Brenda Hillman: "The Shirley Poem,"
Cascadia (Middletown, Connecticut: Weslyan University Press, 2001): 36.

belated and dysphoric. . . Sianne Ngai, Ugly Feelings (Cambridge,
Massachusetts: Harvard University Press: 2005): 331.

"to be / hold the outcast color. . ." Cf. Craig Dworkin: *The Crystal Text*
(Oakland: Compline, 2012): 12.

Strong like a bomb. . . A Tribe Called Quest, "Mr. Muhammed," *People's
Instinctive Travels and the Paths of Rhythm,* Jive Records, 1990.

EXTRACTION

Barbarism colors the entire picture. . . Louis Mumford: *Technics and Civilization*
(New York: Harcourt, Brace and Company, 1934): 73.

> *Technics and Civilization* was published in 1934, at a time when
> 'barbarism' was in widespread use. It meant cruelty, also
> 'primitive' and 'savage', two terms now, along with barbarism,

widely acknowledged to be racist and imperialist. This othering impulse is obvious in barbarism's origin, as in Greek it meant 'non-Greek'. I included it because I felt the Mumford quote was a powerful way to frame the Extraction section, and for its resonance with Walter Benjamin's quote "There has never been a document of culture, which is not simultaneously one of barbarism," which uses the term and refers to the other end of the production chain, with which this book is also concerned (*Theses on Philosophy of History*, 1942).

You're like, Stephanie, duh... Stephanie Young: *Ursula or University* (San Francisco: Krupskaya, 2013).

mindstuff bound to silver & David Brazil: *antisocial patience* (New York: Roof Books, 2015): 13.

"The actual work of mining..." Mumford, *op. cit.:* 67.

"Never expose celluloid..." sainttherese: "What Is Celluloid? A Jewelry Guide," *Ebay*, http://www.ebay.com/gds/What-Is-Celluloid-A-Jewelry-Guide-/10000000004565574/g.html (13 October 2007).

"Ear ornaments in feathers..." et passim, Jack Ogden: *Jewelry* (London: The Intelligent Layman Publishers Ltd., 2006).

"To fail to recognize the ubiquity..." Fred Moten, "Do Black Lives Matter? Robin D.G. Kelley and Fred Moten in Conversation" (paraphrased from my notes), Fundraiser for Critical Resistance, Bethany Baptist Church, Oakland, CA, 13 December 13 2014.

"Rocks can be ..." F.G.H. Blyth and Michael de Freitas: *Geology for Engineers* (London: Elsevier Ltd, 1984).

"The Revolution and its aftermath..." Claire Phillips: *Jewels and Jewelry* (London: Victoria and Albert Museum, 2008).

"ESTAMOS BIEN EN EL REFUGIO…" José Ojeda, quoted in Héctor Tobar: *Deep Down Dark: The Untold Stories of 33 Men Buried in a Chilean Mine, and the Miracle That Set Them Free* (New York: Picador, 2015): 170.

"2 Chainz *but I got a few…*" 2 Chainz, "I'm Different," *Based on a T.R.U. Story*, Def Jam Recordings, 2012.

You got it down when… Digital Underground, "The Humpty Dance," *Sex Packets,* Tommy Boy Entertainment, 1990.

To audience, unnamed cutters… Mei Mei Berssenbrugge: *Hello, the Roses* (New York: New Directions, 2013): 15.

"Mystification … towards fraud…" Kris E. Lane: *Colour of Paradise: The Emerald in the Age of Gunpowder Empires* (New Haven, CT: Yale University Press, 2010).

"Introducing the New Crystal…" Crystal Cruise Line ad.

Prada… Whole page is a survey of *Vogue* ads containing jewels or rhinestones, September 2015.

Afghanistan… Whole page is a failed survey of countries, the gemstones mined in them, current or former colonial occupiers, and the names of miners working in those countries. It is incomplete and inadequate because laborers' names are much more difficult to find than brand names and because the histories of colonial occupation are much more complex than a page-long list can reflect. The attempt at making a second catalogue mapped to the form of the first is a sort of meta-comment on the elisions and oversimplifications of history.

an aesthetics born of meningitis, addiction, rectal cancer Eleni Stecopoulos: *Visceral Poetics* (Oakland, California: ON: Contemporary Practice: 2016).

"ore & gold oh oh" M. NourbeSe Philip: *Zong!* (Middletown, CT: Wesleyan University Press: 2008).

"Police shot dead…" Democracy Now!: "Massacre in South Africa: Police Defend Killing of 34 Striking Workers at Platinum Mine," http://www.democracynow.org/2012/8/21/massacre_in_south_africa_police_defend (12 August 2012).

So I've assembled the following discreditable models… Rob Halpern: *Music for Porn* (Callicoon, NY: Nightboat Books, 2012): 8.

"Feeling absurd and out of place." Lorena Muñoz-Alonso: "On the liberation upon hearing in the intermediate state." *…ment*, Issue 05: Attune…ment (on generation), http://journalment.org/article/liberation-upon-hearing-intermediate-state (2014).

"suggests the possibility of social bonding and violence at the same time." Sianne Ngai (on Juliana Spahr's poem "LIVE"): *Ugly Feelings* (Cambridge, Massachusetts: Harvard University Press: 2005).

"the disinterest of a growing thing…" Robert Duncan: *The H.D. Book*, Edited and with an Introduction by Michael Boughn and Victor Coleman (Berkeley: University of California Press, 2011): 2.

Out of hallowed bodies bred Gerard Manley Hopkins: *Poems and Prose*, Selected and with an Introduction and Notes by W.H. Gardner (New York: Penguin Books, 1985): 47.

Looking forward to what?… Alice Notley: "Anne's White Glove," *Manhattan Luck* (Oakland: Hearts Desire Press, 2014).

The wind her womb awakened… ff (italicized phrases), *The Kalevala: Epic of the Finnish People*, Translated by Eino Friberg (Helsinki: Otava Publishing Company, Ltd., 1988).

"cosmologizing impulse" Nathaniel Mackey: "Gassire's Lute: Robert Duncan's Vietnam War Poems," *Paracritical Hinge: Essays, Talks, Notes, Interviews* (Madison: University of Wisconsin Press, 2005): 10.

"Why do they need to preserve…" Heriberto Yépez: "Confession and Testimony: on the New Berkeley Poetry Conference," *Lana Turner Journal*, http://www.lanaturnerjournal.com/blog/confession-and-testimony-on-the-new-berkeley-poetry-conference (24 December 2015).

But I believe this / city… Alice Notley: *Songs and Stories of the Ghouls* (Middletown, CT: Wesleyan University Press, 2011).

"here, the bush is burning…" *ff. The Five Books of Moses.* A New Translation with Introductions, Commentary, and Notes by Everett Fox. (New York: Schoken Books, 1983).

"in the velvet lining of their casings…" Susan Buck-Morss: *The Dialectics of Seeing: Walter Benjamin and the Arcades Project* (Cambridge, MA: The MIT Press, 1990): 211.

which expands and rises in ranks… ff. Dante: *The Divine Comedy 3: Paradiso.* Italian text with translation and comment by John D. Sinclair (New York: Oxford University Press, 1961): 437, 447.

"Dangle these darlings…" *Vogue*, December 2014.

"No jewelry in the street!" *Vogue*, 1920.

"Becoming is not simple…" Richard Wilhelm: *Lectures on the I Ching: Constancy and Change* (Princeton, New Jersey: Princeton University Press, 1979): 111.

"Crossing the great water…" Ibid: 41-42.

"[Aguilarite] became valuable…" Elizabeth Ferry: *Minerals, Collecting, and Value Across the US-Mexico Border* (Bloomington and Indianapolis: Indiana University Press, 2013): 90.

SETTING

and so prove, / As ornaments oft do, too dangerous William Shakespeare: *The Winter's Tale* (London: Arden Shakespeare, 2006): 1.2.157-158.

"When I look at it, the deep Asscher cuts…" Elizabeth Taylor: *Elizabeth Taylor: My Love Affair with Jewelry* (New York: Simon & Schuster, 2002): 49.

"Make me feel some type of way." Rich Homie Quan: "Type of Way," *Still Goin In (Reloaded)*, Think It's A Game Entertainment, LLC, 2015.

"A limitless universe of forms" *Chasing Ice*, Directed by Jeff Orlowski, Docudrama Films: 2013.

thou schal lose / Thy joy for a gemme *The Complete Works of the Pearl Poet*, Translated with an introduction by Casey Finch, facing-page Middle English texts edited by Malcolm Andrew, Ronald Waldron, and Clifford Peterson (Berkeley: University of California Press, 1993).

RELATION

Baby, when we're grindin' I get so excited. Next: "Too Close," *Related Next*, Arista, 1997.

If I touch it anyhow it will take in my skin / to the blaze of its own imperfections. Clark Coolidge: *The Crystal Text.* (Great Barrington, MA: The Figures, 1986): 90.

I say people. (What?) what you gonna do? Kool & the Gang: "Get Down On It," *Something Special*, Second Decade Music, 1981.

"a time for co-embodiment" Cf. Lisa Robertson: *Nilling: Prose Essays on Noise, Pornography, The Codex, Melancholy, Lucretius, Folds, Cities and Related Aporias* (Ontario: Bookthug, 2012): 76.

"If distribution and circulation are the aspects…" Cf. Jason Read: *The Micro Politics of Capital: Marx and the Prehistory of the Present* (Albany: State University of New York Press, 2003): 49.

"No one should relinquish his [*sic*] duty…" *Bhagavad Gita: A New Translation:* Translated by Stephen Mitchell (New York: Harmony Books, 2000): [18.50].

THE LATTICE

terror ever present / a shitty lattice Ted Rees, forthcoming work from *the soft abyss* (Vancouver, Brittish Columbia: The Elephants, 2018) shared in correspondence.

rocked only by love, hazard, fate, sleeping Lisa Robertson: *3 Summers* (Toronto, Ontario: Coach House Books, 2016).

I saw a hundred little… Dante, *op. cit.:* 317.

And eke a hundred sonnes… I could have sworn this was Chaucer but I can't find the citation, so maybe it's me imitating Chaucer.

Thank you, many beloveds